#2
WALL FLOWERS

50 drawings by Joan Worth

ISBN-13: 978-1548606800
ISBN-10: 1548606804

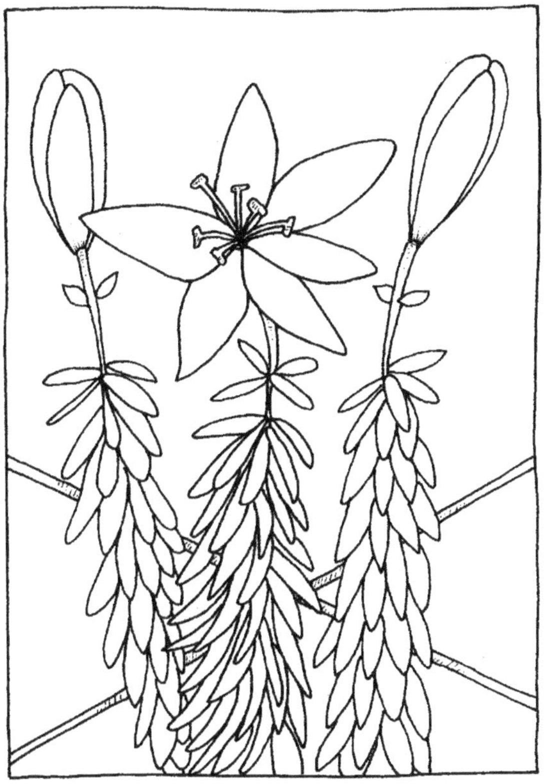

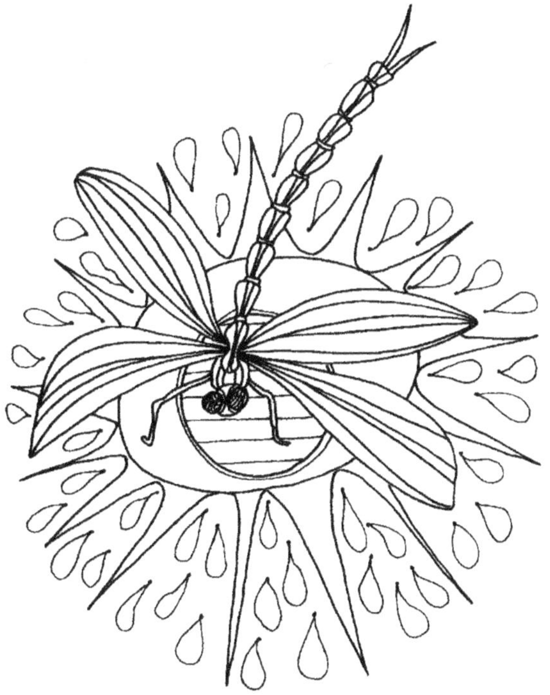

WALL FLOWERS #2 -

WALL FLOWERS #2 - ©2017 Joan Worth

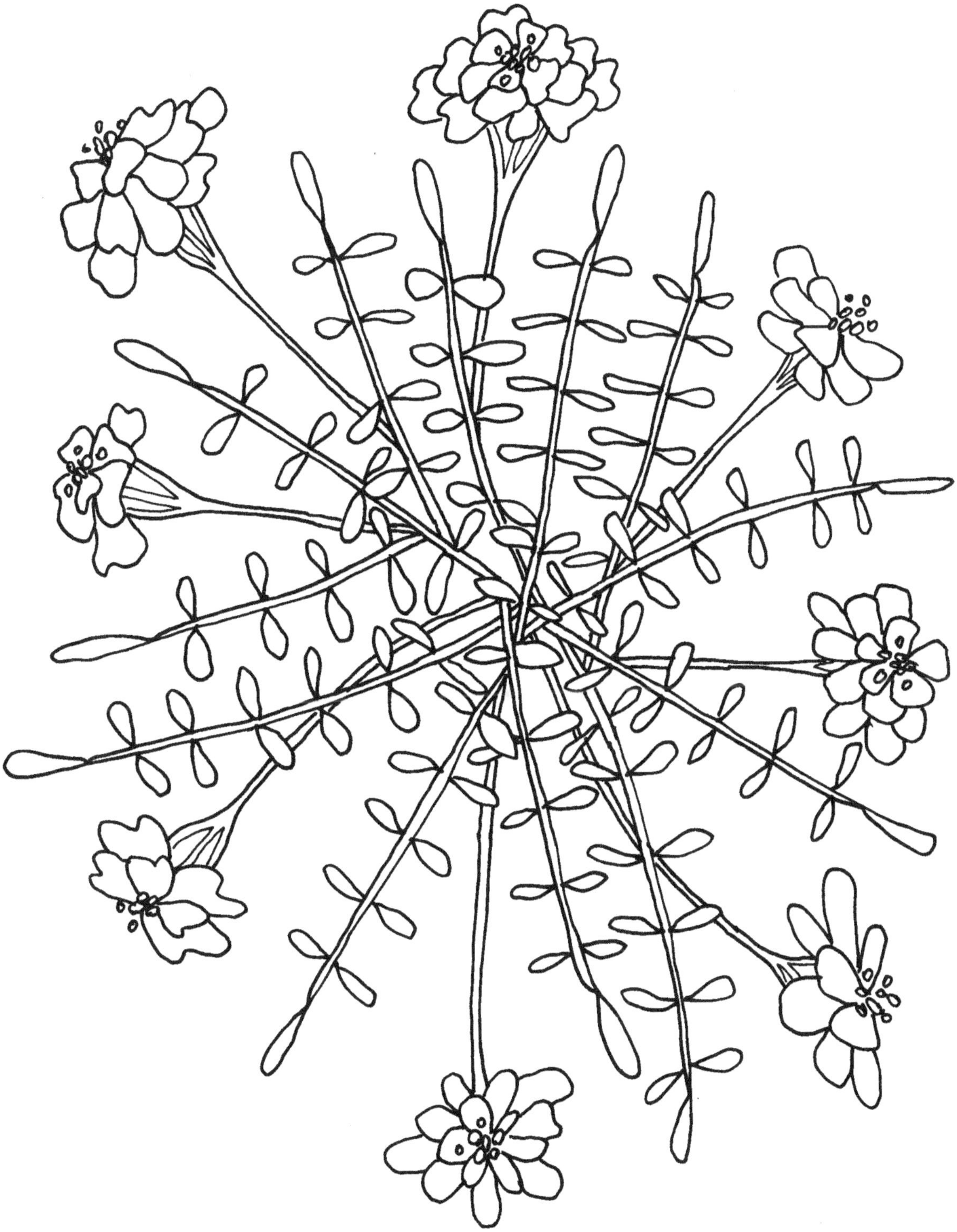

WALL FLOWERS #2 -

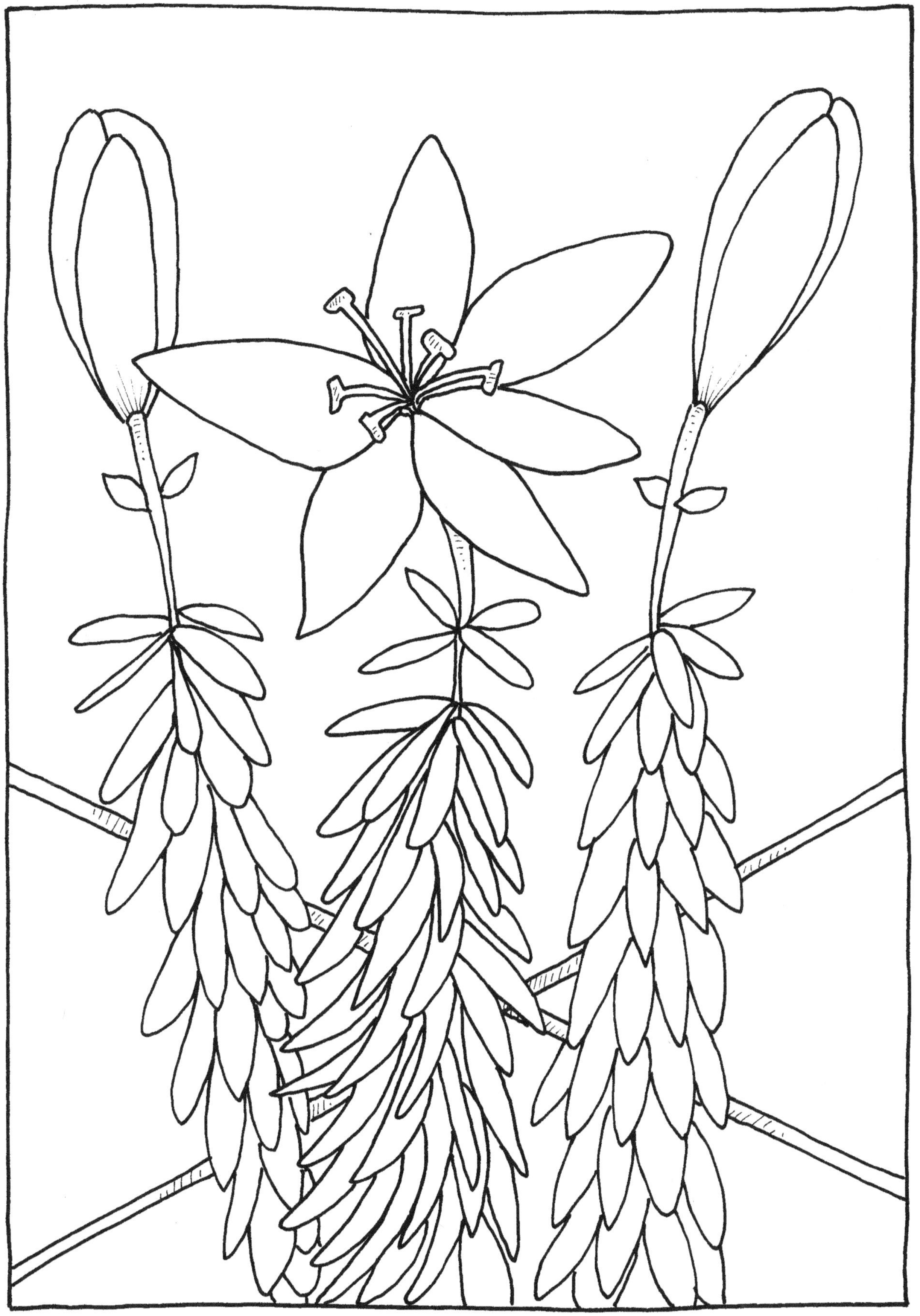

WALL FLOWERS #2 - ©2017 Joan Worth

WALL FLOWERS #2 -

WALL FLOWERS #2 - ©2017 Joan Worth

WALL FLOWERS #2 -

WALL FLOWERS #2 - ©2017 Joan Worth

WALL FLOWERS #2 -

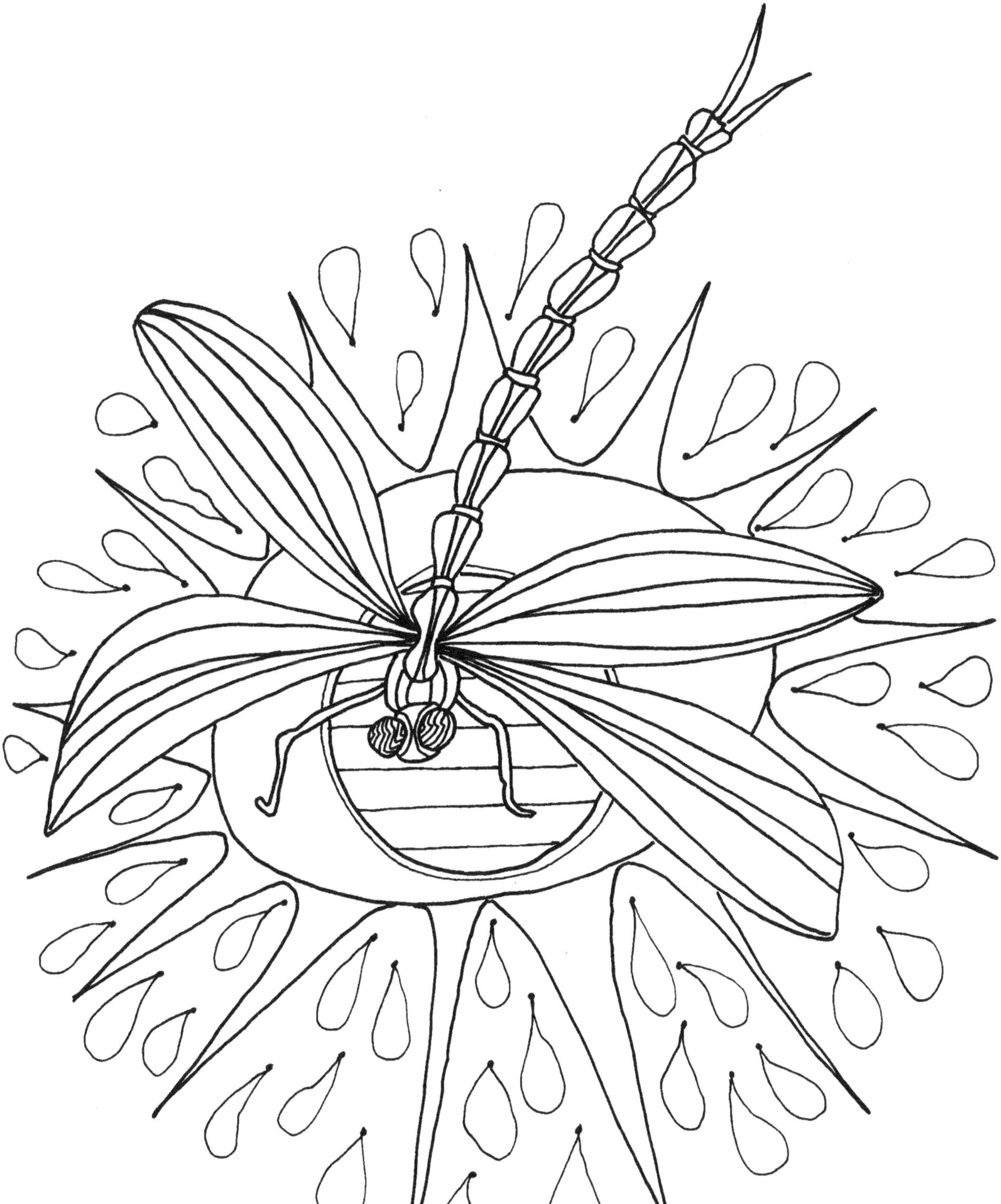

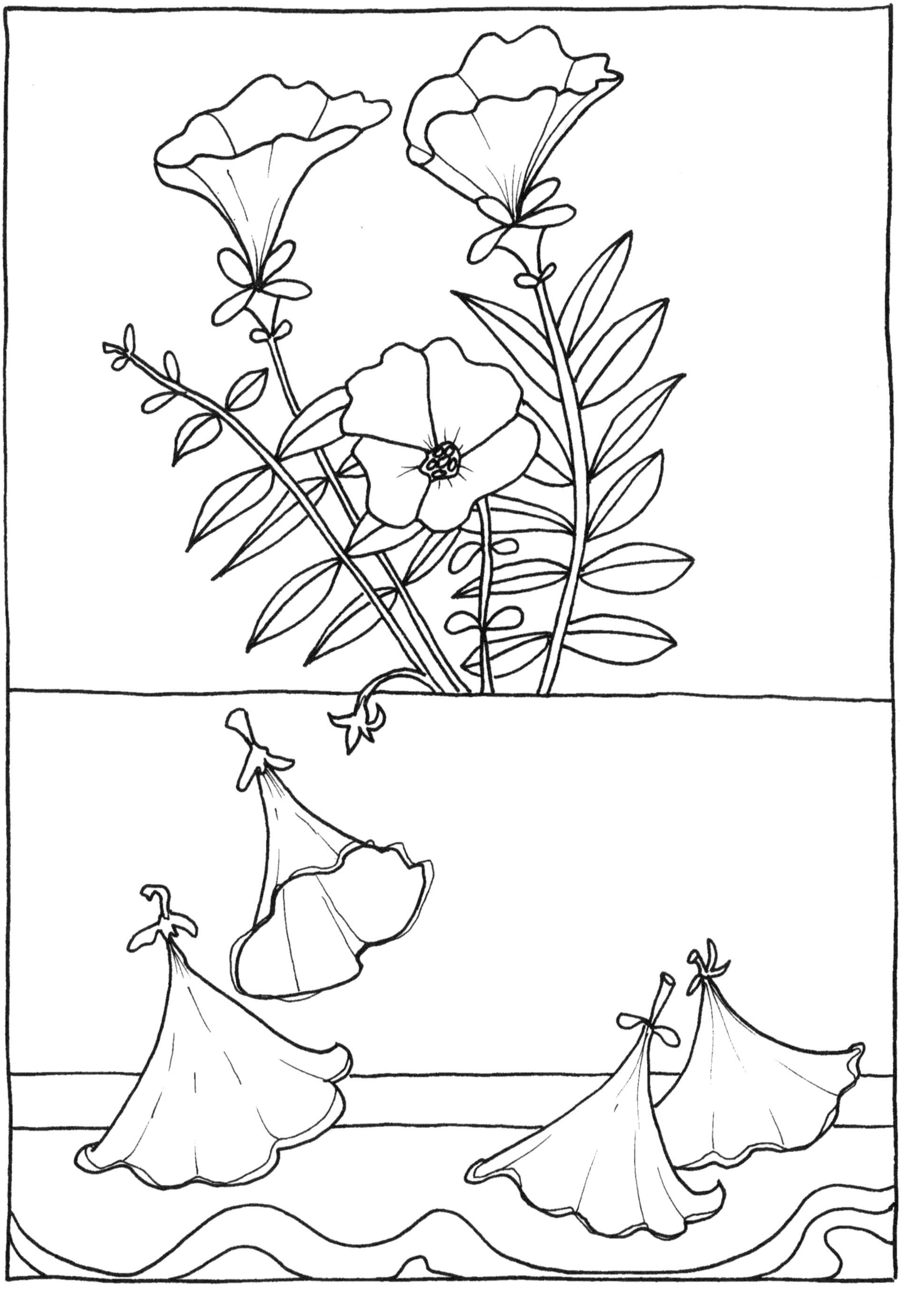

WALL FLOWERS #2 -

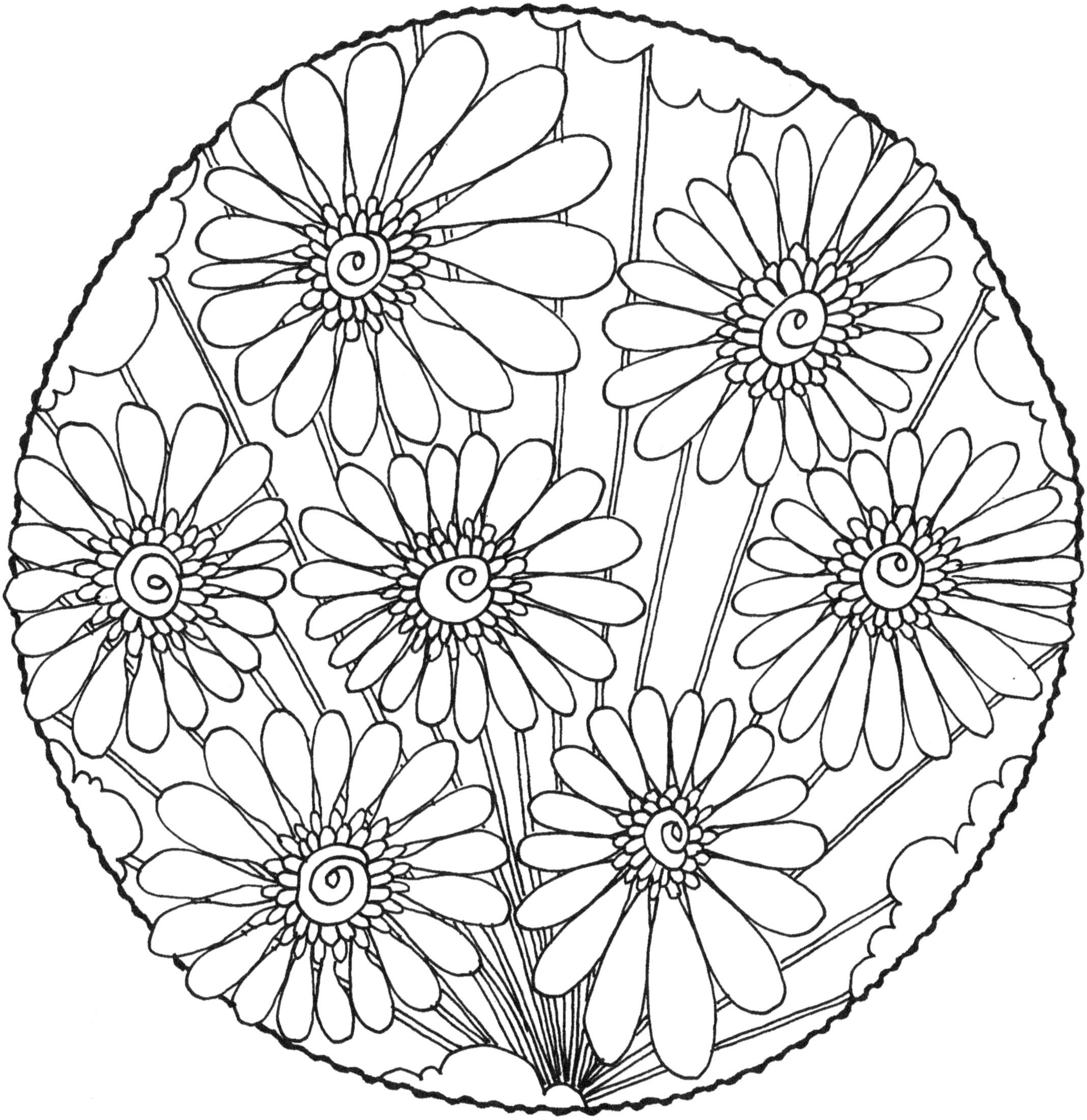

WALL FLOWERS #2 -

WALL FLOWERS #2 -

WALL FLOWERS #2 -

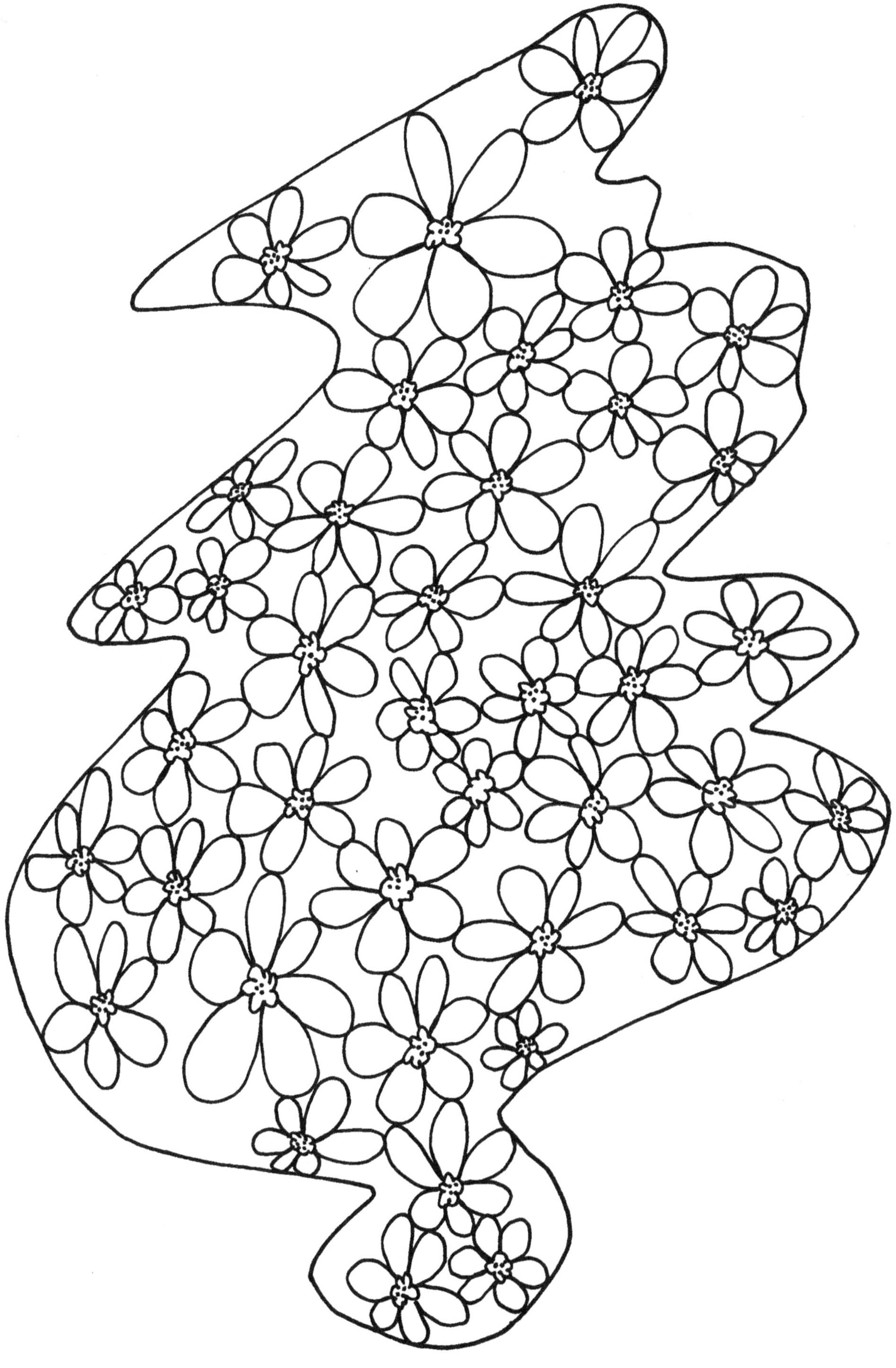

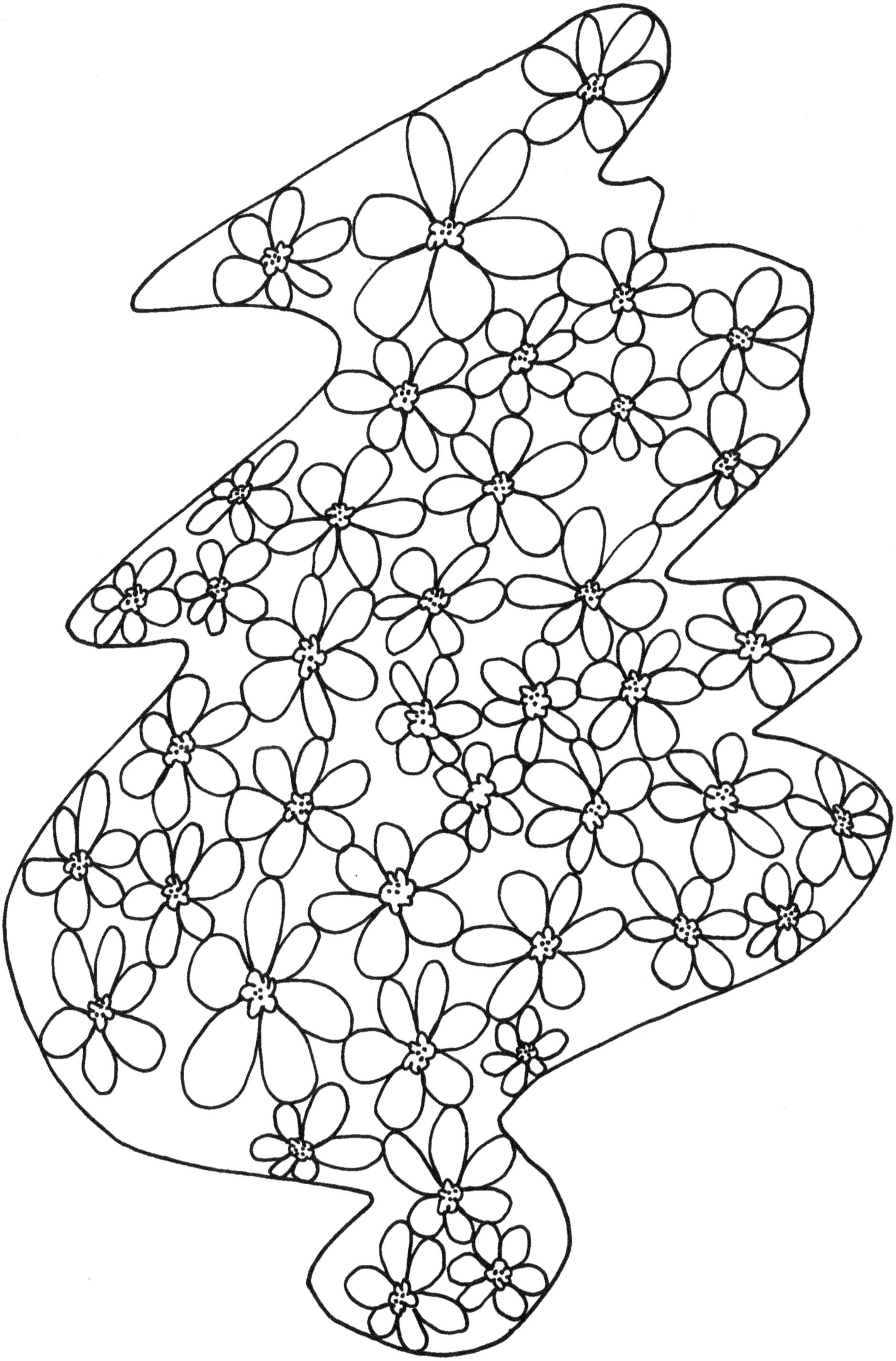

www.ingramcontent.com/pod-product-compliance
Lightning Source LLC
Chambersburg PA
CBHW081223280526
45787CB00006B/2497

* 9 7 8 1 5 4 8 6 0 6 8 0 0 *